Shots

A dazzling guide to the colorful world of layered drinks

MUD PUDDLE BOOKS, INC.
New York, New York

SHOTS: *A Dazzling Guide to the colorful world of layered drinks*

Mud Puddle Books, Inc.
54 W. 21st Street, Suite 601
New York, NY 10010
info@mudpuddlebooks.com

ISBN: 1-59412-100-1

Originally published by
R&R Publications Marketing Pty. Ltd.
12 Edward Street,
Brunswick, Victoria 3054
Australia

© 2004 Richard Carroll

Publisher: Richard Carroll
Mixed Drinks Research: Jon Carroll
Creative Director: Elain Wei Voon Loh
Project Manager: Anthony Carroll
Photography: Warren Webb
Presentation: Jon Carroll
Photography Assistance: Samatha Carroll

Computer Typeset in Avant Garde
Printed in China

table of
contents

introduction   **4**

layering   **14**

shots   **16**

index   **112**

index

After Eight	16	Kool Aid	64
Atomic Bomb	17	Lady Throat Killer	65
B&B Shot	18	Lambada	66
Banana Split	19	Laser Beam	67
Bee Sting	20	Lick Sip Suck	68
Black Nuts	21	Marc's Rainbow	69
Black Widow	22	Margarita Shot	70
Blood Bath	23	Martian Hard On	71
Blow Job	24	Melon Splice	72
Brain Damage	25	Mexican Flag	73
Brave Bull	26	Nude Bomb	74
Candy Cane	27	Orgasm Shot	75
Chastity Belt	28	Oyster Shot	76
Chilli Shot	29	Passion Juice	77
Chocolate Nougat	30	Peach Tree Bay	78
Coathanger	31	Peachy Bum	79
Courting Penelope	32	Pearl Necklace	80
Dark Sunset	33	Perfect Match	81
Devil's Handbrake	34	Pipeline	82
Dirty Orgasm	35	Pipsqueak	83
Double Date	36	Rabbit-Punch	84
Face Off	37	Ready, Set, Go!	85
Fizzy Rush	38	Red Indian	86
Flaming Lamborghini Shot	39	Rusty Nail	87
Flaming Lover	40	Ryan's Rush	88
Flaming Orgy	41	Screaming Death Shot	89
Flaming Sambuca	42	Screwdriver Shot	90
Freddie Fud Pucker	43	Sex in the Snow	91
Fruit Tingle	44	Sherbert Burp	92
Galliano Hot Shot	45	Sidecar Shot	93
Golden Cadillac Shot	46	Silver Thread	94
Grand Slam	47	Slippery Nipple	95
Green Slime	48	Snake Bite	96
Half Nelson	49	Spanish Fly	97
Harbor Lights	50	Springbok	98
Hard On	51	Strawberry Cream	99
Hellraiser	52	Suction Cup	100
High and Dry	53	Suitor	101
Inkahlúarable	54	Sukiyaki	102
Irish Flag	55	Test Tube Baby	103
Italian Stallion	56	The Day After	104
Japanese Slipper	57	T.K.O.	105
Jawbreaker	58	Tickled Pink	106
Jellyfish	59	Towering Inferno	107
Jumping Jack Flash	60	Traffic Light	108
Jumping Mexican	61	U-Turn	109
Kamikaze Shot	62	Vodka-Tini	110
K.G.B. Shot	63	Water-Bubba	111

TECHNIQUES IN MAKING COCKTAILS

1 SHAKE AND POUR: After shaking the cocktail, pour the contents straight into the glass. When pouring into Hi-Ball glasses and sometimes old fashioned glasses the ice cubes are included. This eliminates straining.

2 SHAKE AND STRAIN: Using a Hawthorn strainer (or knife) this technique prevents the ice going into the glass. Straining protects the cocktail ensuring melted ice won't dilute the flavor and mixture.

3 FLOAT INGREDIENTS: Hold the spoon right way up and rest it with the lip slightly above the level of the last layer. Fill spoon gently and the contents will flow smoothly from all around the rim. Use the back of the spoons dish only if you are experienced.

4 FROSTING (sugar and salt rims): This technique is used to coat the rim of the glass with either salt or sugar. First, rub lemon/orange slice juice all the way around only the glass rim. Next, holding the glass by the stem upside down, rest on a plate containing salt or sugar and turn slightly so that it adheres to the glass. Pressing the glass too deeply into the salt or sugar often results in chunks sticking to the glass. A lemon slice is used for salt and an orange slice is used for sugar. To achieve color affects, put a small amount of grenadine or colored liqueur in a plate and coat the rim of the glass, then gently place in the sugar. The grenadine absorbs the sugar and turns it pink. This is much easier than mixing grenadine with sugar and then trying to get it to stick to the glass.

HELPFUL HINTS

Cocktail mixing is an art which is expressed in the preparation and presentation of the cocktail.

HOW TO MAKE A BRANDY ALEXANDER CROSS

Take two short straws and, with a sharp knife, slice one of the straws half way through in the middle and wedge the other uncut straw into the cut straw to create a cross.

STORING FRUIT JUICES

Take a 750mL/25oz bottle and soak it in hot water to remove the label and sterilize the alcohol. The glass has excellent appeal and you'll find it easier to pour the correct measurement with an attached nip pourer.

SUGAR SYRUP RECIPE

Fill a cup or bowl (depending on how much you want to make) with white sugar, top it up with boiling water until the receptacle is just about full and keep stirring until the sugar is fully dissolved. Refrigerate when not in use. Putting a teaspoon of sugar into a cocktail is being lazy, it does not do the job properly as the sugar dissolves.

JUICE TIPS

Never leave juices, Coconut Cream or other ingredients in cans. Pour them into clean bottles, cap and refrigerate them.

ICE

Ice is probably the most important part of cocktails. It is used in nearly all cocktails. Consequently ice must be clean and fresh at all times. The small squared cubes and flat chips of ice are superior for chilling and mixing cocktails. Ice cubes with holes are inefficient. Wet ice, ice scraps and broken ice should only be used in blenders.

CRUSHED ICE

Take the required amount of ice and fold into a clean linen cloth. Although uncivilized, the most effective method is to smash it against the bar floor. Shattering with a bottle may break the bottle. Certain retailers sell portable ice crushers. Alternatively a blender may be used. Half fill with ice and then pour water into the blender until it reaches the level of the ice. Blend for about 30 seconds, strain out the water and you have perfectly crushed ice. Always try and use a metal scoop to collect the ice from the ice tray. Never pick up the ice with your hands. This is unhygienic. Shovelling the glass into the ice tray to gather ice can also cause breakages and hence should be avoided where possible.

It is important that the ice tray is cleaned each day. As ice is colorless and odorless, many people assume wrongly it is always clean. Taking a cloth soaked in hot water, wipe the inside of the bucket warm. The blenders used for all of our bar requirements are Moulinex blenders with glass bowls. We have found these blenders to be of exceptional quality.

GLASSES

Cordial (Embassy)	30mL/1oz
Fancy Hi-Ball Glass	220mL/7oz, 350mL/12oz, 470mL/16oz
Cordial (Lexington)	37mL/1¼oz
Hurricane Glass	230mL/8oz, 440mL/15oz, 650mL/22oz

Tall Dutch Cordial	45mL/1½oz
Wine Goblet	140mL/5oz, 190mL/6oz
Whisky Shot	45mL/1½oz
Cocktail Glass	90mL/3oz, 140mL/5oz
Martini Glass	90mL/3oz
Hi-Ball Glass	270mL/9oz, 285mL/10oz, 330mL/11oz
Margarita Glass	260mL/9oz
Footed Hi-Ball Glass	270mL/9oz, 300mL/10oz
Champagne Saucer	140mL/5oz
Old Fashioned Spirit	185mL/6oz, 210mL/7oz, 290mL/10oz
Salud Grande Glass	290mL/10oz
Fiesta Grande Glass	350mL/12oz, 490mL/17oz
Irish Coffee Glass	250mL/9oz
Fancy Cocktail	210mL/7oz, 300mL/1oz
Brandy Balloon	650mL/12oz
Champagne Flute	140mL/5oz, 180mL/6oz
Poco Grande Glass	380mL/13oz

A proven method to cleaning glasses is to hold each glass individually over a bucket of boiling water until the glass becomes steamy and then with a clean linen cloth rub in a circular way to ensure the glass is polished for the next serve. Cocktails can be poured into any glass but the better the glass the better the appearance of the cocktail. One basic rule should apply and that is, use no colored glasses as they spoil the appearance of cocktails. All glasses have been designed for a specific task, e.g.,

1 Hi-Ball glasses for long cool refreshing drinks.

2 Cocktail glasses for short sharp, or stronger drinks.

3 Champagne saucers for creamy after-dinner style drinks, etc.,

The stem of the glass has been designed so you may hold it while polishing, leaving the bowl free of marks and germs so that you may enjoy your drink. All cocktail glasses should be kept in a refrigerator or filled with ice while you are preparing the cocktails in order to chill the glass. An appealing affect on a 90mL/3oz cocktail glass can be achieved by running the glass under cold water and then placing it in the freezer.

GARNISHES AND JUICES

Banana	Onions
Cucumber	Pineapple
Celery	Orange and Mango
Lemons	Limes
Apple	Olives
Rockmelon	Sugar syrup
Mint leaves	Strawberries
Canned fruit	Cinnamon
Celery salt	Nutmeg
Chocolate flake	Pepper, Salt
Tomato	Fresh milk
Fresh eggs	Sugar and sugar cubes
Fresh single cream	Tabasco sauce
Worcestershire sauce	Oranges
Carbonated waters	Coconut Cream
Lemon – pure	Canned pulps
Canned nectars	Red Maraschino Cherries
Jelly Babies	Crushed Pineapple
Almonds	Red Cocktail Onions
Blueberries	Apricot Conserve
Vanilla Ice Cream	Flowers (assorted)

Simplicity is the most important fact to keep in mind when garnishing cocktails. Do not overdo the garnish; make it striking, but if you can't get near the cocktail to drink it then you have failed. Most world champion cocktails just have a lemon slice, or a single red cherry. Tall refreshing Hi-Balls tend to have more garnish as the glass is larger. A swizzle stick should be served nearly always in long cocktails. Straws are always served for a lady, but optional for a man.

Plastic animals, umbrellas, fans and a whole variety of novelty goods are now available to garnish with, and they add a lot of fun to the drink.

ALCOHOL RECOMMENDED FOR A COCKTAIL BAR

Spirits

Ouzo

Bourbon

Southern Comfort

Campari

Canadian Club

Vandermint

Malibu

Rum

Scotch

Tennessee Whiskey

Brandy

Tequila

Vodka

Gin

Pernod

Liqueurs

Advocaat

Amaretto

Galliano

Banana

Benedictine

Chartreuse – Green & Yellow

Dark Creme de Cacao

Melon

Kirsch

Creme de Menthe Green

Coconut

Sambuca – Clear

Clayton's Tonic (non-alcoholic)

Triple Sec

Drambuie

Cherry Advocaat

Frangelico

Grand Marnier

Bailey's Irish Cream

Kahlúa

Kirsch

Blue Curacao

Mango

Cherry Brandy

Orange

Pimm's

Sambuca – Black

Cointreau

Strawberry

Creme de cafe

Cassis

Peach

Vermouth

Cinzano Bianco Vermouth

Cinzano Dry Vermouth

Cinzano Rosso Vermouth

Martini Bianco Vermouth

Martini Dry Vermouth

Martini Rosso Vermouth

ESSENTIAL EQUIPMENT FOR A COCKTAIL BAR

Cocktail shaker

Hawthorn Strainer

Mixing glass

Spoon with muddler

Moulinex Electric blender

Knife, cutting board

Measures (jiggers)

Can opener

Hand cloths for cleaning glasses

Waiter's friend corkscrew

Bottle openers

Ice scoop

Ice bucket

Free pourers

Swizzle sticks, straws

Coasters and napkins

Scooper spoon (long teaspoon)

DESCRIPTION OF LIQUEURS AND SPIRITS

Advocaat: A combination of fresh egg whites, yolks, sugar, brandy, vanilla and spirit. Limited shelf life, Recommend shelf life 12-15 months from manufacture.

Amaretto: A rich subtle liqueur with a unique almond flavor.

Angostura Bitters: An essential part of any bar or kitchen. A unique additive whose origins date back to 1824. A mysterious blend of natural herbs and spices, both a seasoning and flavoring agent, in both sweet and savory dishes and drinks. Ideal for dieters as it is low in sodium and calories.

Baileys Irish Cream: The largest selling liqueur in the world. It is a blend of Irish Whiskey, softened by Irish Cream and other flavorings. It is a natural product.

Banana: Fresh ripe bananas are the perfect base for the definitive daiquiri and a host of other exciting fruit cocktails.

Benedictine: A perfect end to a perfect meal. Serve straight, with ice, soda, or as part of a favorite cocktail.

Bourbon: Has a smooth, deep, easy flavor.

Brandy: Smooth and mild spirit, is considered a very smooth and palatable, ideal for mixing.

Campari: A drink for many occasions, both as a long or short drink, or as a key ingredient in many fashionable cocktails.

Cassis: Deep, rich purple promises and delivers a regal and robust flavor and aroma. Cassis lends itself to neat drinking or an endless array of delicious sauces and desserts.

Chartreuse: A liqueur available in either yellow or green color. Made by the monks of the Carthusian order. The only world famous liqueur still made by monks.

Cherry Advocaat: Same as Advocaat, plus natural cherry flavors and color is added.

Cherry Brandy: Is made from concentrated, morello cherry juice. Small quantity of bitter almonds and vanilla is added to make it more enjoyable as a neat drink before or after dinner. Excellent for mixers, topping, ice cream, fruit salads, pancakes, etc.

Coconut: A smooth liqueur, composed of exotic coconut, heightened with light-bodied white rum.

Cointreau: Made from a neutral grain spirit, as opposed to Cognac. An aromatic flavor of natural citrus fruits. A great mixer or delightful over ice.

Creme de Cacao Dark: Rich, deep chocolate. Smooth and classy. Serve on its own, or mix for all kinds of delectable treats.

Creme de Cacao White: This liqueur delivers a powerfully lively, full bodied chocolate flavor. Excellent ingredient when absence of color is desired.

Creme de Grand Marnier: A blend of Grand Marnier and smooth French cream. A premium product, a very smooth taste with the orange/cognac flavor blending beautifully with smooth cream.

Creme de Menthe Green: Clear peppermint flavor, reminiscent of a fresh, crisp, clean winter's day in the mountains. Excellent mixer, a necessity in the gourmet kitchen.

Creme de Menthe White: As Creme de Menthe Green, when color is not desired.

Curacao Blue: Same as Triple Sec, brilliant blue color is added to make some cocktails more exciting.

Curacao Orange: Again, same as above, but stronger in orange, coloring is used for other varieties of cocktail mixers.

Curacao Triple Sec: Based on natural citrus fruits. Well known fact is citrus fruits are the most important aromatic flavor constituents. Interesting to know citrus fruit was known 2,000 years before Christ. As a liqueur one of the most versatile. Can be enjoyed with or without ice as a neat drink, or used in mixed cocktails more than any other liqueur. Triple Sec – also known as White Curacao.

Drambuie: A Scotch whisky liqueur. Made from a secret recipe dating back to 1745. 'Dram Buidheach' the drink that satisfies.

Frangelico: A precious liqueur imported from Italy. Made from wild hazelnuts with infusions of berries and flowers to enrich the flavor.

Galliano: The distinguished taste! A classic liqueur that blends with a vast array of mixed drinks.

Gin: Its aroma comes from using the highest quality juniper berries and other rare and subtle herbs. Perfect mixer for both short and long drinks.

Grand Marnier: An original blend of fine old Cognac and an extract of oranges. The recipe is over 150 years old.

Kahlúa: A smooth, dark liqueur made from real coffee and fine clear spirits. Its origins are based in Mexico.

Kirsch: A fruit brandy distilled from morello cherries. Delicious drunk straight and excellent in a variety of food recipes.

Malibu: A clear liqueur based on white rum with the subtle addition of coconut. Its distinctive taste blends naturally with virtually every mixer available.

Melon Liqueur: Soft green, exudes freshness. Refreshing and mouth-watering honeydew melon. Simple yet complex. Smooth on the palate, serve on the rocks, or use to create summertime cocktails.

Ouzo: The traditional spirit aperitif of Greece. The distinctive flavor is derived mainly from the seed of the anise plant. A neutral grain spirit, flavored with anise.

Peach: The flavor of fresh peaches and natural peach juice make this cocktail lover's dream.

Peachtree Schnapps: Crystal clear, light liqueur, bursting with the taste of ripe peaches. Drink chilled or on the rocks or mix with any soft drink or juice.

Pineapple: A just ripe, sun-filled delight. Delicious neat, a necessity for summertime cocktails.

Rum: A smooth, dry, light bodied rum, especially suited for drinks in which you require subtle aroma and delicate flavor.

Rye Whiskey: Distilled from corn, rye and malted barley. A light, mild and delicate Whiskey, ideal for drinking straight or in mixed cocktails.

Sabra: A unique flavor which comes from tangy jaffa oranges, with a hint of chocolate.

Sambuca – Clear: The Italian electric taste experience. Made from elderberries with a touch of anise.

Sambuca – Black: An exciting encounter between Sambuca di Galliano and extracts of black elderberry.

Scotch Whisky: A blended whisky.

Southern Comfort: A liqueur not a bourbon as often thought. It is unique, full-bodied liquor with a touch of sweetness. Its recipe is a secret, but it is known to be based on peaches and apricots.

Strawberry: Fluorescent red, unmistakable strawberry bouquet. Natural liqueur delivers a true to nature, fresh strawberry flavor.

Tennessee Whiskey : Contrary to popular belief, this is not a bourbon, it is a distinctive product called Tennessee Whiskey. Made from the 'old sour mash' process. Leached through hard maple charcoal, then aged in charred white oak barrels, at a controlled temperature, acquiring its body, bouquet and color, yet remaining smooth.

Tequila: Distilled from the Mexcal variety of the cacti plant. A perfect mixer or drink straight with salt and lemon.

Tia Maria: A liqueur with a cane spirit base, and its flavor derived from the finest Jamaican coffee. It is not too sweet with a subtle taste of coffee.

Triple Sec: See Blue Curacao.

Vandermint: A rich chocolate liqueur with the added zest of mint.

Vermouth: By description, Vermouth is a herbally infused wine. Three styles are most prevalent, these are:

   Rosso: A bitter sweet herbal flavor, often drunk as an aperitif.

   Bianco: Is light, fruity and refreshing. Mixes well with soda, lemonade and fruit juices.

   Dry: Is crisp, light and dry and is used as a base for many cocktails.

Vodka: The second largest selling spirit in the world. Most Vodkas are steeped in tanks containing charcoal, removing all odors and impurities, making a superior quality product.

Shots (or pousse-cafes) are perhaps the most eye appealing drinks a barman can produce, especially when they are layered correctly. The secret is in the knowledge of the specific weight of the liqueur used. The lighter ones float on top of the heavier ones. It therefore follows that the heavier ones are poured in first and the lighter ones are then poured progressively according to weight on top, you will then see a distinctive line of each level of colorful liqueurs.

You will have to be very careful when pouring or layering as sometimes the weight of the liqueurs used is very similar and instead of a clear line you will get a very foggy mixture. To make the layering easier it is best to pour each liqueur over the rounded surface of a teaspoon which will have the effect of spreading the liqueur evenly over the one below without mixing. Another method used when the glass is too narrow for a spoon is to insert a glass stirring rod into the glass and then slowly pour each liqueur in turn down the rod. This method, while slow, can be rewarding if similar weighted liqueurs are used. Always be very careful not to touch the inside of the glass while you pour.

As a general rule, the higher the alcohol content of the ingredient the lower the weight of the liquid. If you desire a large number of layers, start with dense alcohol-free syrups like grenadine or coffee flavoring, then finish with sweet cream.

It is important that you layer the drinks in this book exactly in the order given in the recipes.

You can also experiment and make your own beautiful cocktails by using the Liqueur Weight Guide hereunder:

Creme de Cassis (50 proof)	1.18
Creme de Banana (50 proof)	1.18
Anisette Liqueur (red or white 50 proof)	1.17
Creme de Menthe White (60 proof)	1.16
Creme de Menthe Green (60 proof)	1.16
Creme de Cacao (brown or white 50 proof)	1.15
Gold Liqueur (50 proof)	1.15
Kahlua	1.15
Coffee Liqueur (48 proof)	1.14
Maraschino Liqueur (50 proof)	1.14
Creme de Cacao White	1.14
Parfait Amour (50 proof)	1.13
Cherry Liqueur (48 proof)	1.12

Creme de Noyaux	1.12
Strawberry Liqueur	1.12
Blue Curacao (60 proof)	1.11
Galliano	1.11
Amaretto	1.10
Blackberry Liqueur (50 proof)	1.10
Orange Curacao	1.10
Apricot Liqueur (58 proof)	1.09
Cranberry Liqueur	1.09
Tia Maria	1.09
Green Chartreuse	1.09
Dry Orange Curacao (60 proof)	1.09
Triple Sec (60 proof)	1.09
Drambuie	1.08
Frangelico	1.08
Sambuca (clear or black)	1.08
Coffee Flavored Brandy (70 proof)	1.07
Liqueur Monastique (78 proof)	1.07
Peach Flavored Brandy (70 proof)	1.07
Cherry Flavored Brandy (70 proof)	1.07
Blackberry Flavored Brandy (70 proof)	1.07
Apricot Flavored Brandy (70 proof)	1.07
Campari	1.07
Midori Melon Liqueur	1.05
Rye Liqueur (60 proof)	1.05
Ginger Flavored Brandy (70 proof)	1.05
Peppermint Schnappes (60 proof)	1.05
Kummel (78 proof)	1.05
Peach Liqueur (60 proof)	1.05
Sloe Gin (60 proof)	1.04
Benadictine	1.04
Grand Marnier	1.04
Brandy	1.04
Cointreau	1.04
Water	1.00
Tuaca	0.98
Southern Comfort	0.97
Kirsch	0.94
Cream	0.80

after eight

mixers

10mL/^{1}/3fl oz Kahlúa

10mL/^{1}/3fl oz Creme de Menthe

20mL/^{2}/3fl oz Baileys Irish Cream

15mL/^{1}/2fl oz Southern Comfort

method

Pour in order.

technique

Shoot

comments

A peppermint surprise.

atomic bomb

mixers
20mL/²/3fl oz Tia Maria

15mL/¹/2fl oz Gin

10mL/¹/3fl oz cream

method
Layer in order, then float cream.

technique
Shoot

comments
A strategic 'one shot weapon',
this drink explodes down the
unsuspecting throat. Delicious in
emergencies! Gin may be replaced
with Cointreau, or Triple Sec.

b&b shot

mixers

One part Cognac or Brandy

One part DOM Benedictine

method

Pour in order.

technique

Shoot

comments

For mature drinkers! Grandpa can turn up the pace of his medication. The shot is quick and smooth, the traditional B & B cocktail is normally served in a brandy balloon.

banana split

mixers
15mL/¹/2fl oz Kahlúa

15mL/¹/2fl oz Lena
Banana Liqueur

10mL/¹/3fl oz
Strawberry Liqueur

Whipped Cream

method
Layer in order and top with
whipped cream.

technique
Shoot

comments
Let this one slip down sweetly,
with a super strawberry aftertaste.

bee sting

mixers

20mL/^{2}/3fl oz Tequila

10mL/^{1}/3fl oz Yellow
Chartreuse

method

Layer in order, then light.

technique

Straw shoot while flaming.

comments

Ouch! The Yellow Chartreuese
attacks your throat with a numbing,
pleasurable pain, as Tequila buzzes
you back to the party. Drink quickly
so the straw won't melt!

black nuts

mixers
15mL/^{1}/2fl oz Black Sambucca

15mL/^{1}/2fl oz Frangelico

method
Layer in order.

technique
Shoot.

comments
A wonderful `nutty' flavor, with a real anise touch.

black widow

mixers
10mL/^{1}/3fl oz
Strawberry Liqueur

10mL/^{1}/3fl oz Black
Sambuca

10mL/^{1}/3fl oz cream

method
Layer in order.

technique
Shoot

comments
Watch this one, the spider will get
you quickly.

blood bath

mixers

10mL/^{1}/3fl oz Rosso Vermouth

15mL/^{1}/3fl oz Strawberry Liqueur

20mL/^{2}/3fl oz Tequila

method

Pour in order then layer the Tequila.

technique

Shoot

comments

Cherry grins and rosy cheeks characterize the after effects of this blood thirsty experience. Only issued after midnight and before dawn.

blow job

mixers
Two parts Kahlúa

One part Baileys Irish Cream

method
Layer in order and shoot.

technique
Shoot

comments
A light minty confectionery flavor and creamy texture provide a mouthful for those who indulge.

Twist this to a 'Rattlesnake' by adding Green Chartreuse.

brain damage

mixers

20mL/²/3fl oz Coconut
Liqueur

10mL/¹/3fl oz Parfait
Amour Liqueur

5mL/¹/6fl oz Advocaat
Liqueur

method

Layer the Parfait Amour and
Coconut Liqueur, then pour the
Advocaat.

technique

Shoot

comments

Separation induces restless nights.
Advocaat intervenes to mould
the senses.

brave bull

mixers

30mL/1fl oz Crème de Café Liqueur

15mL/¹/2fl oz Tequila

method

Layer in order.

technique

Shoot

comments

One of my favorites for late night revellers, will resist fatigue and maintain stamina. Ad Ouzo and a 'TKO' is punched out.

candy cane

mixers

15mL/^{1}/$_2$fl oz
Grenadine Cordial

15mL/^{1}/$_2$fl oz Creme de
Menthe

25mL/^{5}/$_6$fl oz Vodka

method
Layer in order and shoot.

technique
Shoot

comments
A real candy flavor, with a touch of
menthol.

chastity belt

mixers

20mL/²/3fl oz Tia Maria

10mL/¹/3fl oz
Frangelico

10mL/¹/3fl oz Baileys
Irish Cream

5mL/¹/6fl oz Cream

method

Layer in order, then float the cream.

technique

Shoot

comments

Morality implores you not to succumb to the super-sweet delicacies of drinking's perversity.

chilli shot

mixers
45mL/1¹/₂fl oz Vodka

Slice of red chilli
pepper

method
Pour.

technique
Shoot

comments
Feeling mischievous? Refrigerate
the Vodka with one red chilli
pepper (or 3 to 5 drops of Tabasco
sauce) for 24 hours before serving.

chocolate nougat

mixers

10mL/^{1}/3fl oz
Frangelico Hazelnut
Liqueur

10mL/^{1}/3fl oz DOM
Benedictine

10mL/^{1}/3fl oz Baileys
Irish Cream

method

Pour in order then layer the Bailey's
Irish Cream.

technique

Shoot

comments

A swirling pleasure zone of flowing
Bailey's Irish Cream, above the
finest Benedictine and based with
voluptuous hazelnuts, accentuating
the meaning of chocolate.

coathanger

mixers

15mL/¹/2fl oz
Cointreau*

15mL/¹/2fl oz Tequila

7mL/¹/4fl oz Grenadine
cordial drop of milk

method

Layer Tequila onto the Cointreau,
dash Cordial or Grenadine then
drop the milk.

technique

Shoot, then cup hand entirely over
the rim, insert straw between fingers
into the glass and inhale fumes.

comments

A euphoric experience, quiet
stunning to your senses.

*Cointreau may be replaced with
Triple Sec Liqueur.*

courting penelope

mixers
20mL/²/3fl oz Cognac

15mL/¹/2fl oz Grand
Marnier

method
Pour in order

technique
Shoot

comments
A distinctive acquired taste
is needed for two inseparable
moments!

dark sunset

mixers
One part Dark Crème
de Cacao Liqueur

One part Malibu

method
Layer in order.

technique
Shoot

comments
This tropical paradise reflects
sunset, beaches and the ripe
coconuts of Malibu.

devil's handbrake

mixers

15mL/¹/2fl oz Banana
Liqueur

15mL/¹/2fl oz Mango
Liqueur

15mL/¹/2fl oz Cherry
Brandy

method
Layer in order.

technique
Shoot

comments
A magnificent bounty of fruit
infiltrated by the devil. Exquisite
after a swim.

dirty orgasm

mixers
15mL/¹/2fl oz Triple Sec Liqueur

15mL/¹/2fl oz Galliano

15mL/¹/2fl oz Baileys Irish Cream

method
Layer in order.

technique
Shoot

comments
The Irish frolic between the world's two best lovers, Italian Galliano and French Cointreau. Also known as a 'Screaming Orgasm'. Drambuie may replace Galliano.

double date

mixers

15mL/¹/2fl oz Melon Liqueur

15mL/¹/2fl oz White Crème de Menthe

15mL/¹/2fl oz DOM Benedictine

method

Layer in order.

technique

Tandem

comments

Soothing Crème de Menthe restrains the passion of DOM and Melon. For romantics.

face off

mixers

10mL/^{1}/3fl oz
Grenadine

15mL/^{1}/2fl oz Creme de
Menthe

10mL/^{1}/3fl oz Parfait
Amour

10mL/^{1}/3fl oz Sambuca

method
Layer in order.

technique
Shoot

comments
Too many of these will certainly
cause a loss of face.

fizzy rush

mixers

5mL/^{1}/6fl oz White Crème de Menthe

10mL/^{1}/3fl oz Apricot Brandy

30mL/1fl oz Champagne

method

Pour in order.

technique

Shoot

comments

Bubbles of refreshing Apricot guaranteed to get up your nose.

flaming lamborghini shot

mixers

10mL/^{1}/3fl oz Crème de Café Liqueur

10mL/^{1}/3fl oz Galliano

10mL/^{1}/3fl oz Green Chartreuse

method

Layer in order, then light.

technique

Shoot while flaming.

comments

Get the party into motion. Essential for birthday celebrants.

flaming lover

mixers

15mL/^{1}/2fl oz Sambuca

15mL/^{1}/2fl oz Triple Sec Liqueur

method

Pour Triple Sec over lit Sambuca while drinking through a straw.

technique

Straw shoot while flaming.

comments

The Triple Sec softens the flame for inexperienced drinkers of flaming shots.

flaming orgy

mixers

10mL/^{1}/3fl oz
Grenadine

10mL/^{1}/3fl oz Creme de
Menthe

15mL/^{1}/2fl oz Brandy

10mL/^{1}/3fl oz Tequila

method/ technique
Straw shoot while flaming.

comments
Another of the potent flaming
shots. Don't get your lips too
close to this one.

flaming sambuca

mixers

30mL/1fl oz Sambuca

3 Coffee Beans

method

Pour Sambuca, float coffee beans and light.

technique

Shoot after flame extinguished.

comments

Provides relief from the cold winter. The other way we do it, is to pour Sambuca into a sine glass then light. Cup your hand entirely over the rim while it flames, creating suction. Shake the glass, place under your nose, take your hand from the glass to inhale the fumes, then shoot!

freddie fud pucker

mixers

22mL/²/3fl oz Galliano

10mL/¹/3fl oz Tequila

5mL/¹/6fl oz Orange
Curacao Liqueur

method

Layer Tequila onto Galliano then
drop Orange Curacao.

technique

Shoot

comments

Known to induce dancing on bars
and at beach parties, be sure to
mind you `p's and `f's when
ordering.

fruit tingle

mixers

10mL/^{1}/3fl oz Blue
Curacao Liqueur

15mL/^{1}/2fl oz Mango
Liqueur

5mL/^{1}/6fl oz Lemon
Juice

method

Layer in order, optional to stir.

technique

Shoot

comments

Tangy and piquant. Melon
Liqueur may be substituted
for Mango Liqueur.

galliano hot shot

mixers

15mL/^{1}/2fl oz Galliano

25mL/^{5}/6fl oz Black Coffee

5mL/^{1}/2fl oz Cream

method

Top Galliano with black coffee, then float cream.

technique

Shoot

comments

When in a hurry, a great way to enjoy a liqueur coffee.

golden cadillac shot

mixers

15mL/^{1}/2fl oz White Crème de Cacao

20mL/^{2}/3fl oz Galliano

10mL/^{1}/3fl oz Cream

method

Layer Galliano and White Crème de Cacao, then float cream.

technique

Shoot

comments

Comfort in style is what the distilled cocoa beams give golden Galliano - a real dazzler! The traditional Golden Cadillac cocktail has a larger volume, is shaken over ice and served in a 140mL/5oz Champagne Saucer.

grand slam

mixers

10mL/¹/₃fl oz Lena Banana Liqueur

10mL/¹/₃fl oz Baileys Irish Cream

10mL/¹/₃fl oz Grand Marnier

method

Pour in order, then stir.

technique

Shoot

comments

Banana liqueur with Baileys Irish cream gives a banana smoothie taste. The addition of Grand Marnier has the added flavor of fresh citrus with a kick.

green slime

mixers

20mL/^{2}/3fl oz Melon Liqueur

15mL/^{1}/2fl oz Vodka

5mL/^{1}/6fl oz Egg White

method

Pour in order, then stir.

technique

Shoot

comments

Add more egg white for greater slime. Melon will keep the taste buds occupied, Vodka dilutes the egg white.

half nelson

mixers

15mL/^{1}/2fl oz Crème de Menthe Liqueur

10mL/^{1}/3fl oz Strawberry Liqueur

20mL/^{2}/3fl oz Grand Marnier

method
Layer in order.

technique
Shoot

comments
The referee is unable to break the grip of Strawberry locking its green opponent into an immovable position. For the temporarily incapacitated.

harbor lights

mixers

12mL/¹/3fl oz Kahlúa

12mL/¹/3fl oz Sambuca

12mL/¹/3fl oz Green
Chartreuse

method

Layer in order.

technique

Straw shoot.

comments

Glittering reflections sparkle on
the habor beside a candlelight
dinner. Substitute Yellow Chartreuse
if preferred.

hard on

mixers

20mL/²/3fl oz Creme de Cafe Liqueur

15mL/¹/2fl oz Banana Liqueur

10mL/¹/3fl oz Cream

method

Layer Liqueur onto Kahlua, then float the cream.

technique

Shoot

comments

The first to float cream, voted the most popular shot.

hellraiser

mixers

15mL/¹/2fl oz Melon
Liqueur

15mL/¹/2fl oz
Strawberry Liqueur

15mL/¹/2fl oz Black
Sambuca

method
Layer in order.

technique
Shoot

comments
A hell of a drink!

high and dry

mixers

10mL/^{1}/3fl oz Bianco Vermouth

15mL/^{1}/2fl oz Tequila

5mL/^{1}/6fl oz Dry Vermouth

method
Pour in order, then stir.

technique
Shoot

comments
Disguise the mischief of Tequila with Dry Vermouth. Best served chilled.

inkahlúarable

mixers
10mL/^{1}/3fl oz Kahlua

10mL/^{1}/3fl oz Triple Sec Liqueur

10mL/^{1}/3fl oz Grand Marnier

method
Layer in order.

technique
Shoot

comments
Terminal illness can be momentarily postponed with this Kahlua-based antidote.

irish flag

mixers

12mL/¹/3fl oz Green
Creme de Menthe

12mL/¹/3fl oz Baileys
Irish Cream

12mL/¹/3fl oz Brandy

method

Layer in order.

technique

Shoot

comments

A stroll through verdant pastures.
Brandy may be replaced with
Tullamore Dew-an Old Irish Whisky.

italian stallion

mixers

15mL/¹/2fl oz Banana Liqueur

15mL/¹/2fl oz Galliano

7mL/¹/5fl oz cream

method

Pour Galliano onto Banana Liqueur, then float cream. Optional to stir.

technique

Shoot

comments

This creamy banana ride you won't forget.

japanese slipper

mixers

20mL/^{2}/3fl oz Melon Liqueur

15mL/^{1}/2fl oz Triple Sec Liqueur*

10mL/^{1}/3fl oz Lemon Juice

method

Layer Triple Sec onto the Melon then float the Lemon Juice. Optional to stir.

technique

Shoot

comments

Elegant and refreshing. Precision is required with measurements. To revive failing confidence and replenish that special feeling.

Cointreau may be substituted for Triple Sec.

jawbreaker

mixers
45mL/1¹/₂fl oz Apricot
Brandy

4-5 drops Tabasco
Sauce

method
Pour Apricot Brandy then drop
Tabasco Sauce.

technique
Shoot

comments
Grit your teeth after this shot, then
slowly open your mouth.

jellyfish

mixers
10mL/¹/3fl oz Blue
Curacao Liqueur

10mL/¹/3fl oz Romana
Sambuca

10mL/¹/3fl oz Baileys
Irish Cream

2 dashes of Grenadine

method
Layer in order and pour Grenadine.

technique
Shoot

comments
Watch out for sting at the end of
this slippery shot.

jumping jack flash

mixers

15mL/¹/2fl oz Tia Maria

15mL/¹/2fl oz Rum

15mL/¹/2fl oz Jack Daniel's

method
Layer in order.

technique
Shoot

comments
Thrill seeking Jack Daniel's and his accomplices await this opportunity to shudder your soul.

jumping mexican

mixers
22mL Crème de Café
Liqueur

22mL Bourbon

method
Layer in order.

technique
Shoot

comments
Jump into Mexico's favorite
pastime and bounce back into
the party. For those keen on the
Mexican Hat Dance.

kamikaze shot

mixers

20mL/^{2}/3fl oz Vodka

15mL/^{1}/2fl oz Cointreau

10mL/^{1}/3fl oz Lemon Juice

method

Layer the Cointreau onto Vodka, float the lemon juice, then optional to stir.

technique

Shoot

comments

Maintain freshness for large volumes by adding strained egg white. Mix in a jug and keep refrigerated. The traditional Kamikaze cocktail has the additional of Lime cordial, it is shaken over ice, strained and then served in a 140mL/5oz Cocktail Glass.

Triple Sec may be substituted for Cointreau.

K.G.B. shot

mixers
12mL/¹/3fl oz Kahlua

12mL/¹/3fl oz Grand
Marnier

12mL/¹/3fl oz Baileys
Irish Cream

method
Layer in order.

technique
Shoot

comments
Grand Marnier adds an orange
twist to the Kahlua and Baileys Irish
Cream. The traditional K.G.B.
cocktail is built over ice with greater
volume of ingredient. It is normally
served in a 140mL/5oz Old
Fashioned Spirit Glass.

kool aid

mixers

10mL/¹/3fl oz Melon
Liqueur

15mL/¹/2fl oz Amaretto
di Saroono

10mL/¹/3fl oz Vodka

method

Layer in order.

technique

Shoot

comments

A familiar mix with various
names. Amaretto's caramel lacing
prevents overheating.

lady throat killer

mixers

20mL/²/3fl oz Crème de
Café Liqueur

15mL/¹/2fl oz Melon
Liqueur

10mL/¹/3fl oz
Frangelico Hazelnut
Liqueur

method
Layer in order.

technique
Shoot

comments
This superb mixture offers an
exquisite after-taste. One of
my favorite Shots.

lambada

mixers

15mL/^{1}/2fl oz Mango
Liqueur

15mL/^{1}/2fl oz Black
Sambuca

15mL/^{1}/2fl oz Tequila

method
Layer in order.

technique
Shoot

comments
Wiggle your way to the bar
and order the latest liqueur, Black
Sambuca. Both the dance and
the Shot will excite your partner.

laser beam

mixers

25mL/5/6fl oz Galliano

20m/2/3fl oz Tequila

method

Layer in order and shoot.

technique

Shoot

comments

Your palate is illuminated on this celestial journey!

lick sip suck

mixers
30mL/1fl oz Tequila
lemon in quarters or
slices salt

method
Pour Tequila into glass. On the flat
piece of skin between the base of
your thumb and index finger, place
a pinch of salt. Place a quarter of
the lemon by you on the bar. Lick
the salt off your hand, shoot the
Tequila and then suck the lemon
in quick succession.

marc's rainbow

mixers

8mL/¹/5fl oz Crème de
Café Liqueur

8mL/¹/5fl oz Melon
Liqueur

8mL/¹/5fl oz Malibu

8mL/¹/5fl oz Banana
Liqueur

8mL/¹/5fl oz Galliano

8mL/¹/5fl oz Grand
Marnier

method
Layer in order.

technique
Shoot

comments
One of the best shot recipes.
Discover the pot of gold
at the end of the rainbow.

margarita shot

mixers

15mL/^{1}/2fl oz
Cointreau*

15mL/^{1}/2fl oz Tequila

10mL/^{1}/3fl oz Lemon
Juice

5mL/^{1}/6fl oz Lime Juice

method

Layer Tequila onto Cointreau,
float lemon juice then dash the
lime juice.

technique

Shoot

comments

Everyone should take this plunge.
Lemon and Lime neutralize the
acid. This Shot is similar to the
traditional Margarita cocktail, which
is of greater volume, shaken over
ice and served in a salt rimmed
Champagne Saucer.

*Triple Sec may be substituted for
Cointreau.*

martian hard on

mixers

15mL/¹/2fl oz Dark
Crème de Cacao

15mL/¹/2fl oz Melon
Liqueur

15mL/¹/2fl oz Baileys
Irish Cream

method
Layer in order.

technique
Shoot

comments
When you are a little green about
the facts of life.

melon splice

mixers

15mL/^{1}/2fl oz Melon
Liqueur

15mL/^{1}/2fl oz Galliano

15mL/^{1}/2fl oz Coconut
Liqueur

method

Layer in order.

technique

Shoot

comments

Synonymous with Sunday strolls and
ice-cream. Flakes of ice may be
sprinkled to chill.

mexican flag

mixers
15mL/¹/2fl oz
Grenadine Cordial

15mL/¹/2fl oz Creme de
Menthe

15mL/¹/2fl oz Tequila

method
Layer in order and shoot.

technique
Shoot

comments
Try this 'South of the Border'
flag waver.

nude bomb

mixers

10mL/^{1}/3fl oz Kahlúa

10mL/^{1}/3fl oz Banana Liqueur

10mL/^{1}/3fl oz Amaretto di Saronno

method

Layer in order.

technique

Shoot

comments

Especially created for toga-parties and skinny-dipping.

orgasm shot

mixers

One part Coinreau*

One part Baileys Irish Cream

method

Layer in order.

technique

Shoot

comments

After the first one, you most certainly will want another. The Shot method is different to the traditional Orgasm cocktail, which is a linger drink, built over ice and served in a 210mL/7 oz Old Fashioned Spirit Glass.

Triple Sec may be substituted for Cointreau.

oyster shot

mixers

10mL/^{1}/3fl oz Vodka

10mL/^{1}/3fl oz Tomato Juice

5mL/^{1}/6fl oz Cocktail Sauce (see page 19)

Worcestershire sauce to taste

Tabasco sauce to taste

1 fresh oyster

method

Pour tomato juice onto the Vodka, float the cocktail sauce, dash sauces to taste and drop in oyster.

technique

Shoot

comments

An early morning wake-up call, replenishing energy lost the night before. Also referred to as a Heart Starter.

passion juice

mixers

20mL/²/3fl oz Orange
Curacao Liqueur

10mL/¹/3fl oz Cherry
Brandy Liqueur

15mL/¹/2fl oz freshly
squeezed Orange or
Lemon juice

method

Layer in order. Optional to stir.

technique

Shoot

comments

A bitter sweet lift by garnishing
liqueur passion with juices.

peach tree bay

mixers

25mL/⁵/₆fl oz Peachtree Schnapps

15m/¹/₂fl oz Pimm's No. 1 Cup

5mL/¹/₆fl oz Crème de Menthe Liqueur

method

Layer the Pimm's onto the Peachtree Schnapps, then drop Green Crème de Menthe.

technique

Shoot

comments

Conjuring an image of uninhabited places, cool refreshing Pimm's is minted with Green Crème de Menthe.

peachy bum

mixers
20mL/²/3fl oz Mango
Liqueur

15mL/¹/2fl oz
Peachtree Schnapps

10mL/¹/3fl oz Cream

method
Layer in order.

technique
Shoot

comments
Delightfully enriched and mellowed
by fresh cream.

pearl necklace

mixers

15mL/¹/₂fl oz Melon Liqueur

15mL/¹/₂fl oz Pimm's No. 1 Cup

method

Layer in order.

technique

Shoot

comments

A dash of lemonade dilutes the zappy after-taste.

perfect match

mixers
20mL/²/3fl oz Parfait
Amour Liqueur

20mL/²/3fl oz Malibu

method
Layer in order.

technique
Shoot

comments
Parfaits (Perfect), Amour (Love),
proposes future happiness and
togetherness and under Malibu's
exotic veil.

pipeline

mixers

25mL/^{5}/$_6$fl oz Tequila

20mL/^{2}/$_3$fl oz Vodka

method

Layer in order.

technique

Shoot

comments

Ride the wild surf in this pipeline.

pipsqueak

mixers

20mL/^{2}/3fl oz Frangelico Hazelnut Liqueur

10mL/^{1}/3fl oz Vodka

7mL/^{1}/5fl oz Lemon Juice

method
Layer in order, then stir.

technique
Shoot

comments
Another favorite of mine. A quaint appetizer before dinner.

rabbit-punch

mixers

10mL/¹/3fl oz Campari

10mL/¹/3fl oz Dark
Crème de Cacao

10mL/¹/3fl oz Malibu

15mL/¹/2fl oz Baileys
Irish Cream

method

Pour in order then layer Baileys Irish
Cream.

technique

Shoot

comments

Baileys Irish Cream assures credibility
and its softness will subtly inflict a
powerful jab to wake you up and
keep you on the hop!

ready, set, go!

mixers

15mL/¹/2fl oz
Strawberry Liqueur

15mL/¹/2fl oz Banana
Liqueur

15mL/¹/2fl oz Midori

method

Layer in order and straw shoot.

red indian

mixers

10mL/^{1}/3fl oz Dark
Crème de Cacao

10mL/^{1}/3fl oz
Peachtree Schnapps

15mL/^{1}/2fl oz Canadian
Club

method
Layer in order.

technique
Shoot

comments
Dark Crème de Cacao ripens the
Peachtree to tantalize.

rusty nail

mixers
15mL/¹/2fl oz Scotch Whisky

15mL/¹/2fl oz Drambuie

method
Layer in order.

technique
Shoot

comments
A pillow-softener, though this age-old blend will never cause fatigue. As a Shot, great as 'one for the road'. The traditional cocktail is normally built over ice, in a 210mL/7oz Old Fashioned Spirit Glass.

ryan's rush

mixers

10mL/¹/3fl oz Kahlúa

10mL/¹/3fl oz Baileys
Irish Cream

10mL/¹/3fl oz Rum

method
Layer in order.

technique
Shoot

comments
An easy one. Don't be lulled by
the pleasant taste, this one has
a real kick.

screaming death shot

mixers

15mL/^{1}/2fl oz Crème de Café Liqueur

10mL/^{1}/3fl oz Cougar Bourbon

10mL/^{1}/3fl oz DOM Benedictine

5mL/^{1}/6fl oz Bourbon

5mL/^{1}/6fl oz Bundaberg OP

method

Layer in the above order. Lighting optional.

technique

Shoot while flaming.

comments

The pinnacle of endurance. Double layers of flammable fuel cushioned in ascending order by Crème de Café Liqueur, Bourbon and Benedictine, which sweetly numbs any pain. It's truth and dare.

screwdriver shot

mixers
15mL/¹/₂fl oz Orange
Liqueur

30mL/1¹/₂fl oz Vodka

method
Layer in order.

technique
Shoot

comments
Add a dash of Peachtree Schnapps
and it's known as a `Fuzzy Navel'.
The Shot mix departs from the
traditional Screwdriver cocktail by
the substitution of Orange Liqueur
for Orange juice. The cocktail is also
built over ice in a 210mL/7oz Old
Fashioned Spirit glass.

sex in the snow

mixers
12mL/¹/3fl oz Triple Sec Liqueur

12mL/¹/3fl oz Malibu

12mL/¹/3fl oz Ouzo

method
Pour in order, then stir.

technique
Straw Shoot.

comments
The sub-zero temperature of this combination is chillingly refreshing when drunk through a straw.

sherbert burp

mixers

15mL/¹/₂fl oz
Strawberry Liqueur

30mL/1fl oz
Champagne

method

Pour Strawberry Liqueur then top up
with Champagne.

technique

Shoot

comments

Change the color of your burp with
any flavored liqueur. Even better,
multi-color it!

sidecar shot

mixers
10mL/¹/3fl oz Brandy

15mL/¹/2fl oz
Cointreau*

10mL/¹/3fl oz Lemon
Juice

method
Layer Cointreau onto Brandy, float
Lemon Juice, then optional to stir.

technique
Shoot

comments
This old-fashioned, lemon-barley
refreshment, filtered through
Cointreau and lightly tanned with
Brandy, restores your zest for life.
A slightly different mix to the
traditional Sidecar cocktail, which
is shaken over ice and served in
a 90mL/3oz Cocktail glass.

*Cointreau may be substituted with
Triple Sec.

silver thread

mixers

15mL/¹/2fl oz Creme de Menthe

15mL/¹/2fl oz Banana Liqueur

15mL/¹/2fl oz Tia Maria

method
Layer in order.

technique
Shoot or lick, sip and suck.

comments
A great shot to mend the fences. Try this one on with the oldies.

slippery nipple

mixers

30mL/1fl oz Sambuca

15mL/^{1}/2fl oz Baileys
Irish Cream

method
Layer in order.

technique
Shoot

comments
One of the originals, very well
received. Cream floated on the
Baileys becomes a 'Pregnant
Slippery Nipple'. Grand Marnier
included makes a 'Slipadicthome'.

snake bite

mixers
20mL/²/3fl oz Creme de Cafe Liqueur

10mL/¹/3fl oz Green Chartreuse

method
Layer in order, then light.

technique
Straw shoot while flaming.

comments
Score this shot ten out of ten. Drink quickly or the straw will melt.

spanish fly

mixers

10mL/^{1}/3fl oz Bianco Vermouth

15mL/^{1}/2fl oz Tequila

20mL/^{2}/3fl oz Whisky

method/technique

Tandem

comments

No, it's not what you're twinkling eye and devious smirk assumes... it's better. A guaranteed survival capsule, capable of producing fantasies beyond those Spain is famous for.

springbok

mixers

20mL/²/3fl oz
Passionfruit Syrup

10mL/¹/3fl oz Crème de
Menthe Liqueur

5mL/¹/6fl oz Ouzo

method
Layer in order.

technique
Shoot

comments
Named after the beautiful
Springbok of Africa, formerly a motif
on the South African Rugby jersey.

strawberry cream

mixers
20mL/²/3fl oz
Strawberry Liqueur

10mL/¹/3fl oz Cream

method
Layer in order.

technique
Shoot

comments
Begin your trip to the 'World of
Shots' with this one. Cream acts as
a buffer to entice the nervous and
inexperienced. Strawberries calm
what was needless concern.

suction cup

mixers
20mL/²/3fl oz Vodka

10mL/¹/3fl oz Melon Liqueur

7mL/¹/5fl oz Blue Curacao Liqueur

method
Layer the Melon onto Vodka, then pour Blue Curacao.

technique
Suction-straw shoot.

comments
A supersonic vacuum results from this drinking method.

suitor

mixers

10mL/^{1}/3fl oz
Drambuie*

10mL/^{1}/3fl oz Grand
Marnier

10mL/^{1}/3fl oz Baileys
Irish Cream

7mL/^{1}/5fl oz Milk

method
Pour in order.

technique
Shoot

comments
Milk inclusion coddles a cool
moment, resettles anxieties
when approaching the fair sex,
guaranteed to excite romance.

*Drambuie may be substituted with
Lochan Ora.*

sukiyaki

mixers

10mL/^{1}/3fl oz Mango
Liqueur

10mL/^{1}/3fl oz Apricot
Brandy

10mL/^{1}/3fl oz Malibu

method
Layer in order.

technique
Shoot

comments
Essential starter for s superb
Japanese banquet.

test tube baby

mixers

25mL/⁵/₆fl oz Grand Marnier

20mL/²/₃fl oz Ouzo drop of Baileys Irish Cream

method

Layer in order and shoot.

technique

Shoot

comments

Bubbles of refreshing Apricot guaranteed to get up your nose.

the day after

mixers

10mL/¹/₃fl oz
Cointreau*

10mL/¹/₃fl oz Tequila

5 drops Blue Curacao
Liqueur

10mL/¹/₃fl oz Green
Chartreuse

method

Layer Tequila onto Cointreau. Drop
the Blue Curacao, then layer Green
Chartreuse and light.

technique

Shoot after flame extinguished.

comments

An upside down day!

*Cointreau may be substituted with
Triple Sec.*

T.K.O.

mixers

10mL/¹/3fl oz Kahlúa

10mL/¹/3fl oz Tequila

10mL/¹/3fl oz Ouzo

method

Layer in order.

technique

Shoot

comments

Don't fall with this TKO, drink it with pleasure, recover without pain.

tickled pink

mixers

40mL/1^{1}/3fl oz White
Crème de Menthe

5mL/^{1}/6fl oz Grenadine
Cordial

method

Pour White Crème de Menthe
followed by a dash of Grenadine
or Raspberry Cordial.

technique

Shoot

comments

For those who are bashful when
complimented.

towering inferno

mixers

10mL/¹/3fl oz Dry Gin

10mL/¹/3fl oz Triple Sec Liqueur

10mL/¹/3fl oz Green Chartreuse

method

Layer in order, then light.

technique

Shoot while flaming.

comments

Designed to set the night on fire.

traffic light

mixers
10mL/^{1}/3fl oz
Strawberry Liqueur

10mL/^{1}/3fl oz Galliano

25mL/^{5}/6fl oz Green
Chartreuse

method
Layer in order, light, then light.

technique
Suction-straw shoot.

comments
Ready set go! Substitute Banana
Liqueur for Galliano and Melon
Liqueur for Green Chartreuse,
for those with a sweet tooth.

u-turn

mixers
15mL/¹/₂fl oz Banana
Liqueur

30mL/1fl oz Tia Maria

method
Layer in order.

technique
Shoot

comments
The Banana offers the curve yet
it's Tia Maria that sends you around
the bend. A complete change
of direction.

vodka-tini

mixers

25mL/^{5}/6fl oz Vodka

5mL/^{1}/6fl oz Dry
Vermouth

method

Pour in order, then stir.

technique

Shoot

comments

No olive is required. Preferably
served chilled.

water-bubba

mixers

15mL/¹/2fl oz Cherry
Advocaat

10mL/¹/3fl oz Advocaat

10mL/¹/3fl oz Blue
Curacao

method

Pour Advocaat into Cherry
Advocaat, then layer the Blue
Curacao and shoot.

technique

Shoot

comments

The Advocaat resembles an egg
yolk, with veins of Cherry Advocaat.
Also known as an 'Unborn Baby'.

After Eight	14	Kool Aid	62
Atomic Bomb	15	Lady Throat Killer	63
B&B Shot	16	Lambada	64
Banana Split	17	Laser Beam	65
Bee Sting	18	Lick Sip Suck	66
Black Nuts	19	Marc's Rainbow	67
Black Widow	20	Margarita Shot	68
Blood Bath	21	Martian Hard On	69
Blow Job	22	Melon Splice	70
Brain Damage	23	Mexican Flag	71
Brave Bull	24	Nude Bomb	72
Candy Cane	25	Orgasm Shot	73
Chastity Belt	26	Oyster Shot	74
Chilli Shot	27	Passion Juice	75
Chocolate Nougat	28	Peach Tree Bay	76
Coathanger	29	Peachy Bum	77
Courting Penelope	30	Pearl Necklace	78
Dark Sunset	31	Perfect Match	79
Devil's Handbrake	32	Pipeline	80
Dirty Orgasm	33	Pipsqueak	81
Double Date	34	Rabbit-Punch	82
Face Off	35	Ready, Set, Go!	83
Fizzy Rush	36	Red Indian	84
Flaming Lamborghini Shot	37	Rusty Nail	85
Flaming Lover	38	Ryan's Rush	86
Flaming Orgy	39	Screaming Death Shot	87
Flaming Sambuca	40	Screwdriver Shot	88
Freddie Fud Pucker	41	Sex in the Snow	89
Fruit Tingle	42	Sherbert Burp	90
Galliano Hot Shot	43	Sidecar Shot	91
Golden Cadillac Shot	44	Silver Thread	92
Grand Slam	45	Slippery Nipple	93
Green Slime	46	Snake Bite	94
Half Nelson	47	Spanish Fly	95
Harbor Lights	48	Springbok	96
Hard On	49	Strawberry Cream	97
Hellraiser	50	Suction Cup	98
High and Dry	51	Suitor	99
Inkahlúarable	52	Sukiyaki	100
Irish Flag	53	Test Tube Baby	101
Italian Stallion	54	The Day After	102
Japanese Slipper	55	T.K.O.	103
Jawbreaker	56	Tickled Pink	104
Jellyfish	57	Towering Inferno	105
Jumping Jack Flash	58	Traffic Light	106
Jumping Mexican	59	U-Turn	107
Kamikaze Shot	60	Vodka-Tini	108
K.G.B. Shot	61	Water-Bubba	109